Rob Gee qualified as a psychiatric nurse in 1994 and worked for twelve years in mental health units around the UK and Australia before becoming a stand-up poet. He's performed at a hundred fringe festivals across the world and won numerous poetry slams, including the Edinburgh Slam, the Arts Council's Lit Up Slam, BBC Two's Why Poetry Matters Slam and the Orlando Poetry Smackdown. He's received over twenty awards for his solo shows.

Rob is patron of Leicestershire Action for Mental Health Project (LAMP) and lead artist for the Comedy Asylum: comedy shows written and performed by people receiving mental health treatment. He returned to nursing during the COVID-19 pandemic.

Many of the events depicted in the poems are true and every effort has been made to represent them without distortion or exaggeration. However, for reasons of confidentiality and respect, any details which might identify anyone involved have been altered or removed.

Paul & Helen,

Enjoy!

The Day My Head Exploded

Rob

xx

Poems about Healthcare
1993 - 2020

Rob Gee

Burning Eye

BurningEyeBooks
Never Knowingly
Mainstream

This edition published by Burning Eye Books 2021

www.burningeye.co.uk

@burningeyebooks

Burning Eye Books
15 West Hill, Portishead, BS20 6LG

ISBN 978-1-913958-00-8

The Day My Head Exploded

Also by Rob Gee:
Forget Me Not: The Alzheimer's Whodunnit
Kevin, King of Egypt
My Daughter Is a Donington Goth
Pig on the Wall

Anthology of group poems:
Word Round: Poems from Psych Wards

For Shaib Kurmoo,
psych dad to so many of us

CONTENTS

Foreword	13
Introduction	15
A Very Chilled Robbery	17
A Hug	20
The Kindness of Paul	21
The Day My Head Exploded	22
Cassandra's Mantra	26
Home	27
Cassandra's Handover	28
Chronic Obstructive Pulmonary Disease Singalong	32
Elsie's Letter	34
Play the Fool Who's Fooling You	37
The Boy with the Staples	39
Exercise Poem for Older People	40
If… (Nursing Mentorship Remix)	42
Medication	45
Duncan's Jab	47
The Messiah	49
Our Loss	50
Human Carpentry	51
Done a Bad Thing	52
Squaddies	53
Herman's Habit, Part 1	54
The NHS: A History	56
I'm on a Section, Get Me Out of Here	59
Dementia Champions Poem	60
The Boxer	63
Simone's Bag	65

'You Don't Have to Be in This Much Pain, You Know…' 67
Romeo the Policeman 68
Nursing Psychopaths 69
Swear to Be Happy 71
Superpower 73
Whisky in Your Tea 75
Psychiatric Crash Team 76
My Eyes 78
Herman's Habit, Part 2 79
Herman's Habit, Part 3 80
Dr Brice 82
Tom's Love Story 83
Ducks 88
My Kingdom for a Swipe Card 89
Fight in the Old Dog 90
A Man Re-evaluates 92
The Andrew Lansley Rap 94
Richard's Leaves 97
Lockdown Haiku 99
Post-Meal Lockdown Poem 100
Little Victories 102
Leaving 104
Night Out 106
Reflections on COVID 108

Abbreviations and Terms 115

'In theory there is no difference between theory and practice, while in practice there is.'

Benjamin Brewster, *Yale Literary Magazine*, February 1882

FOREWORD

This collection is a perfect synthesis of comedy, theatre and poetry. The humour catches you off guard and allows subject matters to be introduced that might otherwise be too difficult to approach. It conveys and illuminates the realities of nursing – as encountered over the last twenty-seven years to date, predominantly in the UK but also beyond. It's political without being obvious and it's autobiographical in a way that has a public, very relevant, dimension. The gallows humour is underpinned by a tenderness and compassion; a perfect balance of horror and humour, pathos and absurdity.

I have come into contact with many people who've been nursed by Rob. Again and again, they mention him positively, as someone who understood and was able to make a traumatic inpatient experience a lot more bearable. What I find most refreshing about him is his natural understanding of the therapeutic power of the creative arts, as well as his capacity to see his patients as people, rather than mental health problems. From a professional but also personal perspective, I know this to be true. Many years ago I met Nurse Gee as a patient. I left him as a poet.

Lydia Towsey
Poet and performer (*The Venus Papers*, *The English Disease*)
Arts in Mental Health coordinator, Leicestershire Partnership NHS Trust

INTRODUCTION

In the 1950s my great-aunt Ada and her sister Freda both immigrated to the UK from Ireland and commenced careers as mental health nurses. I didn't start my training until 1991, by which time they had both retired. I'll never forget the combination of mirth and pity in their eyes when I told them I was going into the profession.

By the early 1990s, the institutions built in the Victorian era were starting to close. Long-stay patients were being moved out into 'the community', while people with immediate mental health concerns were now treated in acute units. Nursing also started to become more academic in its efforts to be taken seriously as a profession. Whenever I discussed the job with my aunts it was apparent how much our role had changed. It's changed again since.

Several poems here represent a snapshot of adult mental health nursing at the turn of the millennium. Since then, wards have become smaller and single-gender, smoking has been banned and uniforms have returned. The last of these would have pleased my aunts immensely, whereas I hardly ever wore a uniform in my career.

Some poems here are from my days as a student nurse. Others are from a more critical perspective and they were written later, by an older me. Several are from my time working as a writer in healthcare settings and a few are from the COVID-19 crisis, when I returned to nursing.

There's also the title piece, loosely based on my experience of being hospitalised with meningitis. I would like to take this opportunity to thank the staff at the Leicester Royal Infirmary for a high-quality inpatient experience, as well as for discharging me with a bottle of liquid morphine, without which that particular poem would never have been written.

Finally, thank you for reading, buying, borrowing, scanning or photocopying this book. I love you all.

Rob, November 2020

A VERY CHILLED ROBBERY

He'd been in the institution for a number of years.

One day in the 1980s,
he and his mate were chatting
and one of them asked a question
which ultimately changed everything:

'What would they do if we robbed a bank?
Surely, given that the state has incarcerated us
on the basis that we're insane,
if we were to rob one and get caught,
we wouldn't legally be to blame.

'And, if we were to plead insanity,
wouldn't they then be obliged to accept the plea?
Surely the worst they can do is send us back here.
Given the nature of our current medical and legal circumstances,
how can this possibly be a bad idea?'

So they buy two clown masks and two water pistols,
which they paint black in their occupational therapy session.
Then, having gained the appropriate level of trust and permission,

they catch the bus into town,
walk into a bank and hold it up.
It goes really well,
due, partly, to luck,

but mainly to the fact
that the tellers aren't remotely traumatised,
because they're being robbed by two guys
who are clearly holding water pistols,

and who, furthermore, have been enormously polite,
having both stood patiently in line

with their masks on,
waiting for a teller.
It takes decades of institutionalisation
to go into that kind of behaviour.

So the cashiers all decide
that they might as well comply
with the bank's policy of erring on the side of caution,
making this the most laid-back bank robbery of all time,
where neither robbers nor victims
really care about the conclusion.

So they duly hand over the cash,
which our two heroes then stuff into two plastic bags.
They say cheerio to the tellers and leave the bank,
lift up their clown masks and hail a cab,

in which they make their getaway
to the pub around the corner,
fifty yards away.

They walk in
and order a round for everyone there,
much to everyone's liking,
and thus begins the biggest impromptu piss-up
that part of the world has seen
since the days of the Vikings.

Word spreads
and by sundown the boozer is full of people,
all of whom are transcendentally plastered
on the bank's money.

When the armed police finally arrive,
they find these two, completely pie-eyed,

sat at a table with the masks
and a big pile of cash,
going, 'One for you, one for me,
one for you, one for me...'

They were put on separate wards after that.

Summer 1997

A HUG

A hug can make you feel at home.
It can soothe a broken soul
and help you feel less alone.

A hug can let the warmth in
when you're chilly or reclusive.
Hugs are often better than drugs,
but they're not mutually exclusive.

Autumn 2018

THE KINDNESS OF PAUL

He came to my house to see how I was feeling.
I was feeling pretty rotten. I was still reeling
from the catastrophe that had happened to my brain.
I was feeling very mortal
and terrified that nothing would ever be the same.

All I wanted to do was sit at home in the snug
and let the telly be content.
He then came round every week to take me out,
which I have to say I couldn't but resent.

But as time went by,
he slowly reintroduced me to life,
and now I do what I do to the best of my ability.
I love swimming,
because it takes all the weight off my body,
and I'm no artist,
but painting gives me an easy tranquillity.

I'm not working now, but it's not game over,
and if death decides to come for me,
it won't find me a pushover.

I'd have spent the rest of my life in fear in that chair
if Paul hadn't brought me here
and taken me there,

so if you ever see him, please buy him a beer.
Tell him it's from Glyn, and that I'm still here.

*Writer in residence, art group for people with strokes and
head injuries, winter 2016*

THE DAY MY HEAD EXPLODED

The day my head exploded,
I woke up with a headache quite late in the morning.
It was a bit of a surprise,
'cause I hadn't been drinking
the night before.
I'd been sitting at home,
feeling a bit bored.

There was nothing to do and I didn't feel quite right,
so I took myself to bed and had an early night.

Then I woke with this pain behind my eyes,
like an incessant throbbing.
I started sobbing,
'cause I'm a bit of a wuss.
I staggered to the mirror
and my whole head was covered in pus.

Then it started growing before my eyes,
like a balloon being slowly inflated.

I ran outside
while I could still squeeze it through the door,
legged it to the shop across the road,
slid along the floor
and up to the counter.

'Wow,' the bloke said.
'You've got a really massive head.
It's like a big wobbly cyst.
It's not a newsagent you need, mate.
It's a chemist.'

I bought some ibuprofen off him anyway,
'cause it's an anti-inflammatory.
Then I ran down the road to the nearest pharmacy.

'Your head's expanding,'
said the chemist as I staggered in.
'I can't help you.
What you need is a doctor with a very sharp pin.'

I groaned and ran outside.
My head was now three feet wide.

I made my way to my GP surgery
as fast as my head would let my legs carry me.
I was living through the worst of my fears.
Small children were looking at me and bursting into tears.

I reached the waiting room not a moment too soon.
Up to the counter I bravely strode,
but the receptionist had all the social skills
of a neglected commode.

'You can't have an appointment for today,' she said,
'expanding head or no expanding head.
You should have rung the surgery promptly at 8.30am.

'I can fit you in a week after Thursday next,
at ten past six in the morning.
It's a popular slot,
so don't miss the appointment or you'll be shot.
You won't see anyone before then at this surgery.
Maybe you should go to A&E.'

I crowbarred my head outside,
resisted the urge to cry,
pulled out my phone and called 999.

Then I sat and waited for two hours by the side of the road.
I wasn't feeling any better.
My head was now five foot in diameter,
and my boils were oozing this cranial oil.
I looked like a leaking alien.

Then these paramedics rolled up
and said, 'Alas and alack,
we'll never fit your head in the back.
Our only course of action, if you approve,
is to put you next to the lights on the roof
and secure you up there with some sort of strap.'

So they drove through the streets with me on board.
The frost froze my head like a genital wart,
but at least it stopped growing temporarily
until we reached the entrance to A&E.

They took me inside
and told me to wait in line,
where I was robustly ignored for a really long time.

All the while my head kept growing.
It started to make a creaking sound,
and there was no way of knowing
when it was going to stop.
I looked at the clock.

Then a doctor appeared
and said, 'Hello. I'm a locum.
I've been on duty for a very long time
and I've no idea what I'm supposed to be doing.
Now, apparently you've got a head that won't stop growing?'

Without looking up from his notes,
he checked my pulse and diagnosed:
'Well, that seems to be normal.
I suggest you go home and take some paracetamol.

'Try and have an early night,
and if it's no better in the morning, go and see your GP.
Oh, and take some ibuprofen, 'cause it is an anti-inflammatory.'

Then my head exploded.

Everyone in the surrounding area
was covered in blood, goo, teeth,
chunks of cranium, embarrassing memories,
long-forgotten secrets and bits of grey matter.

The health-related posters on the wall
were spattered with my innermost thoughts.
An eyeball popped into a nearby lady.
I accidentally waterboarded a newborn baby.

The doctor took it very personally.
'Well,' he said, 'that was antisocial.
We have a zero-tolerance policy towards exploding patients.
From now on you'll have to vent your frustrations
away from A&E.
In future, try and conduct yourself with a bit more dignity.'

So now I'm back in my flat,
trying to grow a new head from scratch.
It's taken a while, but it's starting to appear.
I'm just waiting for the nose and a couple of ears.

And it might sound optimistic,
but if my next head is super handsome,
it might just be worth it,
and if not,
I'll just make do with whatever I've got,

and if my next head gets bigger at any juncture,
I'll just go straight for acupuncture.

Spring 2012

CASSANDRA'S MANTRA

When you're feeling low
and life has got you licked,
and all your loved ones have to offer
is self-righteous detritus;

when you're in your own company
and your face still doesn't fit,
and life has kicked the living shit
out of your happy-ever-afters;

when you endlessly pull your soul apart
for every last mistake,
and you've drunk so much cheap alcohol
your liver feels like a swollen pancake;

when no one can find or help you
in your own private hell,
you might want to consider
a career in mental health...

Summer 1999

HOME

People gravitate to mental health for all sorts of reasons.
I was paid for going to sleep.

The week of my eighteenth birthday,
I took a job in a psychiatric home.
I'd be there all night,
on my own,
giving out meds
without supervision.

I never thought it might be dodgy.
It was a lovely place for them and me.
There was always lots to eat
and a good-sized television.

Every week I'd be paid in cash.
There was a room upstairs where I'd crash,
and the daytimes were mine to call my own.
That was how mental health happened to me:
sleepover shifts in a care home.

The residents were ten fellas
who'd spent decades in the institution,
and, now it was closed,
they were exposed to a world
that didn't have time for their kind of wisdom.

The atmosphere was like a supportive family.
We'd stay up late and watch the telly.
I'd have endless conversations with them.

Back then I didn't realise
how much they took me under their wing.
We ate trifle, smoked fags and drank coffee all night.
We'd natter about anything.

We'd eat spaghetti on toast and then go to bed,
and then someone told me this was called nursing.

Autumn 1994

CASSANDRA'S HANDOVER

Hello, everyone. Shut up. Get a pen.
Newsnight's on soon, I want to be home by then.

Your first new admission is Daniel Farmish,
or Dan, to his friends
– if he had any.
He's a forty-year-old Falklands War veteran
with post-traumatic stress disorder.
He's got flashbacks and nightmares,
he's riddled with guilt
and his wife died on Wednesday.

He's in after a carbon monoxide attempt.
He was found by a jogger
and he's a little bit snippy.
He has made it known that he wants to go,
but we think the gas has knackered his memory,

so we're going to hang on to him
and assess him for a bit,
and he's not going to like it,
but that's tough shit,
so he's not to leave the ward
unless there's another fire in the dormitory.

Bronwen is a cackling bundle of fun and frivolity;
Ben's psyche is unravelling
like the thread on a crap cardie.

Shona's slowly coming down,
Joan is alright.
Inderjit is on leave
and Terry is getting high.

He's had triple helpings at dinner and breakfast,
he's got eyes like burst raspberries
and he's grinning like an idiot.
Oh, and he stinks of weed.

And I'm sorry to leave you in the lurch,
but he still needs a search
and I've not had the opportunity,
'cause I've been processing Paranoid Andrea
and Dan, the suicidal ex-squaddie with PTSD.

Duncan is insane to the point of barking.
He's convinced it's all an international experiment.
All in all, he seems to be coping,
but he's not washed in a few days
and he's starting to ferment.

Ruth has gone on leave.
Well, I sent her on leave.
She isn't quite ready, but we needed her bed.
I gave her the option of sleeping on Ward 4 for a bit,
and she said that she'd rather eat her own shit,
and that's pretty damning, because she is anorexic.

She's refused all her meals
and she's still feeling faint,
but I've packed her off home
and her mum's made a complaint.

Nathan thought herpes was a small town in Belgium
and gonorrhoea's a boat that you punt around in Venice.
I've assured him that they're not and he's got them both,
which is why he's on antivirals and antibiotics.

Amy is on leave; Jess is a disaster.
I had to move her out of that dormitory,
because it reached the point
where they all wanted to kill her.

So I've put her in Brenda's room,
which obviously means that I've had to move Brenda,
but I couldn't put her in Jess's dorm,
'cause she and Shona don't get on,
so I've put her in Marion's bed and relocated Marion,
who's now in Jess's old bed and she's not very pleased,
but she's not my patient, so I don't give a monkey's.

Simone is the hero of the hour.
She's not self-harmed since Monday's little mishap.
There's still that chunk of cup unaccounted for,
but I don't feel inclined to get in a flap.

Jack Haggerty's back.
He's been taking crack.
He's in, he's paranoid,
it's all a bit daft.

It turns out he's been selling it
to half the people in the outpatients unit,
as well as a couple of catering staff.

He's convinced that he's Jesus,
come down to save us all from sin,
but he's been heavily sedated,
so you won't hear from him.

Anita Bagshaw is still the most likely to do herself in.
She's lower than a rattlesnake's arse,
but she's got that smile that's not reassuring.

Victor's on leave for another week still.
We've not heard anything,
so he's either dead or doing well.

Mark is now free of alcohol.
He's finished his detox,
so he's for the off.
He's discharging himself after ward round in the morning,
so by lunchtime he'll be happily off his box.

Tom – he's the bloke who chopped his hand off.
His wife and kids are coming in tomorrow evening
and he's shitting himself,
so he could probably do with seeing.

Samantha's quite scary,
but don't let her threaten yer;
Margaret will need her blood pressure doing,
and don't forget Robert's morning enema.

Sandra seems to be softening;
Suzie is shite;
Jasmine's quite chipper;
Jenny's had an early night.
Doug's still fairly seedy;
Marion's being needy;
I've not seen Isobel all shift,
but I think she's alright,
and as for Jake Macready,
his outlook on life is God's own mystery.

Rachel is on leave, but she might ring you in the night,
and Martin tried to pull his front teeth out earlier,
but apart from that he's doing alright.

So that's your merry lot
and, now they're offloaded,
I'm going home to get happily loaded.

Toodle-oo and good luck.
There's quite a few things I've missed out,
but you've got all night and you can always read up.

I'm pleased to be off for the next few days,
because I think it is fair to say
that your fan is beginning to whirr
and the shit is on its way.

Hurray!

Adult mental health, summer 1999

CHRONIC OBSTRUCTIVE PULMONARY DISEASE SINGALONG

to the tune of the Tom Jones song 'Delilah'

I wake up my whole street with my cough in the morning.
I have a hack like a cat that just swallowed a frog.
I struggle breathing,
But now that I'm singing
I'm finding the strength to go on.

My, my, my Delilah,
You help me respire.
I could see my own mortality,
But now that I'm singing my voice has just set me free.

Groundbreaking research has shown that singing can help you
(*Da da daaaaaa…*),
Reduces stress and puts oxygen into your blood
(*Da da daaaaaa…*),
Helps your wellbeing
(*Ha ha ha ha ha ha*),
If laughter's the best medicine
Then singing is almost as good.

My, my, my emphysema
Makes my phlegm so much greener,
So, before we can't sing any more,
Raise your voice to the heavens
And let's give the angels what for.

(Solo)

I sound like Muttley
(*Heh heh heh heh heh heh*).
When I ring my poor mum
It sounds like a dirty phone call.

My, my, my emphysema.
The air was once so much cleaner.

So, before we can't breathe any more,
Raise your voice to the heavens,
'Cause that's what your lungs are there for.
Raise your voice to the heavens,
'Cause that's what your lungs are there for.

Written for the Leicester City Clinical Commissioning Group (CCG), winter 2013. The brief was to write a singalong that expounded the merits of choral singing in mitigating symptoms of COPD.

ELSIE'S LETTER

To whom it may concern,

I've never been known for my attention span.
In fact, my husband thinks I'm gormless.
But I'm losing my memory,
one story at a time,

and at the moment I'm getting away with it
in a forgetful kind of way.
I'm trying to keep things in the front of my mind
and I've only left the gas on a couple of times
so far, that I'm aware of,
today.

Now, it just so happens
that I spent a good chunk of my life
working as a nurse in dementia care,
so, although I've no idea where it is my brain's going,
I'm under no illusions
as to what's waiting when it gets there,

So I'd thought I'd better write this letter
for later on in my dementia,
and if you're the sorry sod who's reading it,
then my arse is your career.

I have half a sugar in my tea
and I'm very partial to custard.
I can't abide fisherman's pie,
especially when it's pre-digested.

You can swear in front of me
and I probably won't mind.
Don't worry if you're careless now and again,
as long as you're gentle and kind.
You can even take the piss a little if you like,
'cause I'll be giving you plenty of mine,

but don't treat me like an embarrassment
even when I'm embarrassing.
Just keep me nicely medicated
and clap your hands if you see me singing.

Please don't manhandle me,
unless I hit you first.
Try and make sure I have clothes that fit me
and don't worry about being a brilliant nurse.
Just give me a lie-in now and again
and, if I've filled my nappy
but I appear quite happy,
change the other people first.

And please be gentle with my husband.
We've been married since 1963
and every pore in his body
is going to want to stay with me,
and, although he'll be full of anger and pride,
he'll be quietly going to pieces inside,
so try and involve him as much as you can,
because he does try his best
and he's only a man.

So thanks in advance
for all your hard work and dedication.
I hope I can make you smile as my senses slide,
and I hope that I'm a model patient.

I am aware
the fact I'll lose my memory
won't stop me feeling things emotionally,
so smile a lot, have fun
and lie to me.
When I finally lose it all,
please give me somewhere soft to fall,
so I can decompose with a modicum of dignity;
and, if you have an ounce of compassion,
try and slip me the occasional whisky.

I think that completes the briefing.
I wish you well in all you do,
and if you're ever in my position,
I hope someone does the same for you.

Winter 2012

PLAY THE FOOL WHO'S FOOLING YOU

No matter what your walk of life –
taster of jam,
purveyor of ham,
or a prisoner serving twenty-five to life;
traffic warden, dog groomer, zoologist,
shepherd of the lamb,
or any kind of therapist –

don't forget to use your fool
as your emotional stool.
They don't teach you this at school,

but with your fool as your friend
you can go round the bend
and pretend
everything is fantastic.
Make your heart elastic,

'cause foolish makes you godly-wise,
like a deity in a nappy,
making everybody happy.

For a starter,
change your name to Frank Siddhartha
and sing with a swing,
if that's your thing.

Sit on the floor in a custard wig;
use a knife and fork to dig;
lick a frozen lamppost;
wear a dress made of toast;
ride around on a pot-bellied pig.

Talk French to a dog;
get married to a log.
Don't be harassed to feel embarrassed.
Do what makes you feel convivial.

Fart loudly on a jog.

We recommend wearing melons.
Everywhere you go, just tell 'em:
being good to your inner fool
helps your cerebellum.

Ignore any warning to be sensible,
because taking things too seriously
is simply reprehensible.

So don't think twice – or even once.
Being very silly is good for your bonce.

Group poem written with mental health inpatients,
spring 2018

THE BOY WITH THE STAPLES

He lifted his eyelid
and shot two staples into his pupil.
He didn't want to do it.
He doesn't think he's ill.

They've plagued him since his eighteenth birthday,
and now they're in control, they say
he has to throw himself under a train,
or a car, if he sees one on his way
to the station.

We took him to the infirmary,
where they pulled the staples from his eye
and told him he shouldn't have done it,
as if that hadn't crossed his mind.

He's snoring now, post-op.
It's my job to stay here and stop
him when he wakes and tries to leave,

because, even though he wants to live,
he'll throw himself on that track
to try and make them happy,
so they're no longer on his back.

I'm going to explain
that I'm here to protect him
from what they're telling him to do.

But it's not much in the way of a cavalry:
just little old me
and a Section 3,
and I can't reach those voices.

Royal Infirmary, spring 1995

EXERCISE POEM FOR OLDER PEOPLE

If your lungs creak in your sleep
and wake up before you in the morning,
and you cough up half your soul
before you've finished yawning,
it might be that exercise isn't what you do,
but there'll be a way of keeping fit
that's tailor-made for you.

You can exercise in your chair
with arms and legs and wrists.
You can do it at the hairdresser's
and you can do it at the dentist's.

You can exercise your lungs
by shouting at the telly.
You can exercise your diaphragm
by dancing with your belly.

You can learn about your posture
to improve your mobility
and reduce the number of times
that you exercise with gravity.

You can exercise your finances
and apply for pension credit.
You can cut down on your council tax
and fatten up your wallet.

And when you're in the supermarket,
you can exercise your eyeballs
by having a good close look
at what's written on the labels.

You can exercise your mind
by arguing all the time
with as many people as possible,
especially if you're right.

You can exercise your muscles
and swing your grandkids round,
and you can exercise your assertive skills
by refusing to put them down.

You can improve your circulation
by walking from time to time,
and you can exercise your smile
by sitting in the sunshine.

You can exercise your endorphins
by laughing every week,
and you can exercise your heartbeat
just by dancing cheek to cheek.

*Written and performed at Nottingham City Council's Stay
Healthy conference for older people, autumn 2007*

IF... (NURSING MENTORSHIP REMIX)

If you can introduce your student to their placement properly,
In a way that makes them feel welcome and happy;
If you can design the off-duty rota
To give them decent shifts,
So they're less likely to chuck sickies;

If you can keep in touch with the Trust's education leads,
Respond to each student's specific needs,
And make them realise they're a vital part of the team,
Even though they're supernumerary;

If you can give them the chance
To make some of the mistakes that you did
And take them through the implications of Health and Safety
So they don't accidentally do anything stupid,

And, if they're being a bit of a turkey,
You can break the news to them early,
In a way that makes them feel like they're being supported;

If you can lead the primary, intermediate and final interviews,
Let them get stuck in
And give them stuff to do;

If you can keep everything jargon-free,
Provide teaching sessions
And familiarise yourself with the procedures of the university;

If you can let students participate in ward rounds
And learn to hold their own with the medics;
If you can involve them in decision making,
And get them to deliver some handovers while they're at it;
If you can get them to articulate
Not just what they're doing,
But also their reasons for doing it;

If you can assess them against a set of criteria;
If you can encourage them to learn from each other;
If you can share articles of interest
And simultaneously become familiar
With all the documents of student assessment;
If you can work with your student as often as possible,
While keeping in mind your own professional development;

If you can treat any mistakes as a learning curve
And encourage your student to be discerning;
If you can help them look critically at the evidence
And create an environment conducive to learning;

If you can establish their knowledge base,
Then continuously feed it;
If you can manage them properly
Whenever they're struggling,
And find support for yourself when you need it;

If you can encourage self-reflection,
And read everything you can
About best practice and innovation;

If you can encourage them to underpin the work they do
With reference to guidelines and research too,
As well as various monitoring reviews;

If you can give them a dilemma or two,
And ask what they'd do if they were you;
If you can ask for feedback and give it back;
If you can monitor activities and contribute
To the nursing curriculum
And celebrate good practice,
Especially when it comes from them,

Then you will be a nurse mentor, my friend.

So go forth,
And always remember

That, whether you're evaluating research
Or applying an enema,
You can involve your students
And give them a chance to be the best
Generation of nurses we've ever seen yet:
Compassionate, intelligent and superbly resourced,
And able to make a good cuppa, of course.

So nurture and nourish all the new blood,
And don't forget to fail them if they're no bloody good.

Written and performed at Coventry and Warwickshire NHS Trust's 'Beyond the Horizon' nurse mentorship conference, spring 2011

MEDICATION

The drug trolley yawns open in front of me
and I'm at the helm.
My fingers glide, Liberace-like,
over the boxes and bottles
of antibiotics and hypnotics,
preparations and syrups,
laxatives and vitamins,
pharmacological pick-me-ups,
popping different combinations
into plastic cups
and presenting each one
to the string of humanity lined up
in front of me.

Tom, who severed his hand,
wants lorazepam,
'cause he's panicking
about having a panic attack.
Dan the suicidal ex-squaddie sinks a sleeping tablet
and slowly slopes off to slump into his sack.
Ben has sertraline to stop his brain unravelling,
and Terry the Stoner
is clearly self-medicating.

Samira is checking where everyone is,
and Feisal's at the desk.
Nursing assistants – worked here for years –
and being the nurse in charge when they're on duty
is like riding a crap bike
with a great pair of stabilisers.
They're the most unshockable people I've ever met
and their dickhead receptors are really well calibrated.

Nearly everyone has something at night time,
even if it's only a vitamin.
That's thirty potential drug errors,
and I'm trying to concentrate
while everyone's talking.

There's fluoxetine, olanzapine,
quetiapine and lamotrigine,
sulpiride and chlordiazepoxide,
temazepam and trifluoperazine;
sodium valproate and diazepam,
lithium and lorazepam,
erythromycin and amoxicillin,
carbamazepine and clonazepam,
with lactulose and Maalox to wash it all down,

And that's just for Duncan…

Adult mental health, summer 1999

DUNCAN'S JAB

Duncan hears voices wherever he goes,
and it pisses him off
that everyone else pretends not to hear them.
He and I have a good working rapport
and today he's due his fortnightly injection.

With me is James, our student nurse.
He's a sponge made of keen,
but he's terrified of needles.
He's never given an injection before.
Duncan and I both understand how he feels;

Duncan has kindly allowed James to administer his.
James is discreetly aghast at this,
but he knows he can't back out,
or he'll never become a nurse.
Also, he's only too aware
that if he accidentally jabs the sciatic nerve,
Duncan will be irreparably paralysed for life
and I'll be collecting my P45.

The upper-outer quadrant of the backside
is where the needle goes in.
Hit the centre of that right
and you'll miss the sciatic nerve by quite a safe margin.

Duncan has been having these injections for years,
so his upper-outer quadrant is as tough as old leather.
James is going to have to give it quite a stab.
Duncan's acting all blasé, to help him feel better.

But James's hands are noticeably shaking.
Then he plunges the needle into Duncan's skin,
without giving me the chance
to double-check what he's doing.

Duncan shrieks and hits the deck.
I give a gasp, James nearly drops dead,
while Duncan writhes,
holding his backside.
James looks like he's about to cry.

He's holding the syringe,
with the medication still in.
I attend to Duncan,
who looks up at me with a wolfish grin.

Then he springs to his feet.
'Only joking!'
I could have punched him.

Adult mental health, summer 1999

THE MESSIAH

He sits with His back to a soft lilac wall
and cherishes the dry food on His beard
with a woollen tongue.

Mumbling about the triumphs and mistakes of the past,
His mouth opens without a sound as He silently laughs
to Himself at the absurdity of His situation.

His stained fingers cradle a cigarette,
smoked down to the filter; dead.
His stomach protrudes offensively from a swollen shirt
and His leg vibrates
with an excitable conviction of its own.

Two thousand years ago,
they appeased Him
with the satisfaction of martyrdom.
Today He is frustrated by the arrogance of disbelief,
and miracles are out of the question
when you're on antipsychotic medication.

In the nursing office,
the care-tired staff mull ponderously over His case history:
the grandiose ideas and auditory hallucinations,
religious ideation and perceptual responses.
Jesus has a problem with His neurotransmitters…

but no one can explain the holes.

First acute placement, spring 1993

OUR LOSS

She ligatured herself and died.
We didn't get to her in time.
The grief went through the ward like a horrific ripple.
She was only nineteen, but she was here for so long,
her parents were asking us what song
we thought she'd have liked at her funeral.

Adult mental health, spring 2005

HUMAN CARPENTRY

If you are in your sixties or seventies,
they give you a stainless steel hip,
which is guaranteed for thirty years.
If you're in your eighties or above,
you get a plastic hip,
guaranteed for ten years.

Rubber ants clad in green
crawl in and out of the gap.
She's oblivious to their labours
as she lies on her back,
exhausted, after two long years
crawling up from the bottom of a waiting list,
and, looking at her gaping leg,
my own begins to twitch.

I spoke with her yesterday.
She said it sounded ridiculous,
but she was fond of the old hip
that chased the wind with her
on drunken nights of youth
and had danced in endless circles
around lusty amber halls,
blissfully caressing the hips of others.

Now it cripples her with pain
in its knackered demise;
they're going to replace it
with a virgin piece of plastic.

Human carpentry replaces the parts
that Mother Nature cannot reach,
but two years is a long time
to spend hobbling on your memories.

Orthopaedics, spring 1993

DONE A BAD THING

The Greek student nurse who I sent to pharmacy
for some fallopian tubes
has yet to forgive me,
but the patients were amused,
so at least I did it therapeutically.

Adult mental health, autumn 1996

SQUADDIES

There's a street for ex-soldiers from all generations,
from Suez to Bosnia, by way of the Falklands.

It's serene and peaceful,
with a green in the middle.
Everyone leaves their door off the latch
and every handshake hides a private smile.

It's the kind of place you could imagine as heaven,
if you lived in the fifties
and had no imagination.

There's barely a scream,
when it's daylight, at least,
and the nights are submerged in alcohol and Valium.

Residents make their bed in the morning
with a precision that comes from years of training.
Not many of them ever see the doctor
and pitifully few are still with their wives.

Some have become adept over the course of the years
at making small talk with the emergency services,
but the sight of an argument can move them to tears
and they all lock their windows on Bonfire Night.

Some have hung on to some kind of weapon,
although the only thing they fight for now is their pension,
and to maintain some kind of rapport with their children.
None of them think they'll be going to heaven,

and that's what haunts the look in the eyes
of those who've seen chance toss a coin with their lives,
and, as long as we're happy
to send more to replace them,
we should wear our poppies with shame,
not pride.

Remembrance Day, 2005

HERMAN'S HABIT, PART 1

The first time I met Herman,
he'd broken two policemen's noses simultaneously.

He'd hoovered a silo of speed and ended up in the cells.
It was clear to the constabulary that he wasn't very well.

Two of them had walked in to transfer him to us
and Herman dropped them both.
They put him in cuffs
and he was on the ward within the hour,
black and blue,
his nose spread round his face like a snuffling flower.

He had a broken collarbone and an abrasion or two.
The policeman in charge sort of knew
that we don't take kindly to people hurting our patients,
so he tried to mitigate the evidence with the following statement:

'He was squatting on the toilet,
and he just dived face-first onto the floor.
He didn't even put his hands out to try and break his fall,
and that's how he sustained all those injuries.'

I felt a little bit cynical about this.

Then Herman recovered
and verified it was true:

'Yep! I was all over the place.
I dived face-first off the toilet
and, to my surprise,
I landed on my face.

'They beat me up as well,
but they didn't put their hearts into it.
I think they felt sorry for me
but sort of felt they had to.

It was what you would call a token kicking,
which, I have to say, I think was fitting…'

Adult mental health, winter 2001

THE NHS: A HISTORY

We trained hard, but it seemed that every time we were beginning to form up into teams we would be reorganised. I was to learn later in life that we tend to meet any new situation by reorganising; and a wonderful method it can be for creating the illusion of progress while producing confusion, inefficiency and demoralisation.

Many attribute this quote to Gaius Petronius
in the year 66 AD,
whereas it was Charlton Ogburn Junior
in the late 1950s,

by which time the NHS was barely ten years old,
born in post-war austerity.
At a time when Great Britain was skint,
there was a civilised wish to treat people fairly,
so free healthcare for all became the order of the day,
despite some resistance from the BMA.

By the early 1950s there were some problems with funding,
so prescription charges were reluctantly brought in.
New drugs came on the market in the 1960s,
which added to the costs,
so as to pay the drug companies.

There was a comprehensive reorganisation in 1974,
when services provided by the local authorities
were restructured under regional health authorities,
who were theoretically accountable to me and you,
until they were restructured again in 1982.

Margaret Thatcher took the reins for a spell.
That went well.

The system of consensus management was abolished,
and she introduced the internal market,
where health authorities would purchase care.
This was heavily criticised by Tony Blair,

who adopted the policy when he came to power.
He encouraged outsourcing to the private sector,
and his big legacy was to give
us the Private Finance Initiative,
as well as the National Programme for IT,
which ended up being such a huge mess
it made the Titanic look like a raging success.

The NHS reached an all-time high
in public satisfaction in 2009,
but Dave Cameron said it was second-rate
and had to update,

so a plan was announced to put private companies
at the heart of government policy,
which is like putting King Herod in charge of a crèche facility.

Hospitals sponsored by supermarkets
could convert your care to cash.
Your therapist could be sponsored by GlaxoSmithKline,
getting right behind teen suicide until they were fined,[1]
with your liver transplant brought to you by Smirnoff,
and obs and gynae by Tampax.

In a wave of protest, the proposals were scrapped,
and we were all sidetracked
by a referendum,
which swept through the country in a blizzard of lies,
and as we look to the future,
it seems clearer
than the glazed look in Jeremy Hunt's eyes[2]

that budgets will continue to be squeezed,
while we're expected to meet the needs
of an ageing population
who've had their public services dismantled.

1 To find out more, put the words 'GlaxoSmithKline', 'Paroxetine', 'suicide'
and 'children' into the search engine of your choice.
2. The health secretary at the time of writing

We have a disillusioned workforce
and an attack on junior doctors
that was hideously handled,

and our NHS – the one we have left –
is still cherished by the nation,
because, somewhere among the remnants
of a post-war dream
that my parents rattle on about
when they've not had their medication,
we have a service based on need
that will always exist
as long as there are enough people out there
with the faith to fight for it.

There'll be a debate post-Brexit,
and we can all join in.
The woman with obesity issues is warming up,
but she hasn't started singing.

Spring 2017

I'M ON A SECTION, GET ME OUT OF HERE

It all went wrong, 'cause I wanted a kiss.
I asked for one from my psychiatrist.
He said no, suggested I think.
Then he filled out a form.
The colour was pink.

It said I was failing to keep myself safe
and that I need to be in a unique kind of place
for an assessment period of twenty-eight days,
which may get longer,
to the tune of another five months.
I got cross and called him a…
something I shouldn't.

Which didn't exactly help the cause.
As soon as I was through the doors,
I was struck by the artificial light
and the need for wallpaper.
'What have I done?' I asked myself later.

And no one replied,
because I don't hear voices.
As time went by,
I discovered my choices
were limited to fuck-all,
and it felt quite cruel.
The food is gruel

and it stays in your colon for a week.
The staff sometimes see me,
and we get to speak
about why I can't leave.

All I want now is a little bit of peace;
to sit on my own and relax with a beer.
Now it feels ages till I'll ever be free,
'cause I'm on a section – get me out of here.

Group poem written with mental health inpatients,
summer 2018

DEMENTIA CHAMPIONS POEM

Volunteers and champions! Thank you
for all the extraordinary things you do
every day
as you support people on the journeys they take.
You share the joy, grief, anxiety and laughter.
You help with expectations.
You absorb people's anger.

You don't see illnesses, or patients,
but the person inside.
Every ending needs a start and a middle,
just as everyone's journey requires a guide.

So today
we celebrate
so much good practice,
from advocating for the frail
and the frailty scale
to the safe wandering area and café at the LRI,

normalising incontinence and reducing those stigmas,
making sure people eat with their glasses and dentures,
having toilets that are easy to reach and clearly signed.

We've learned how consistency, calmness and routine
can make all the difference between care and caring.
We've learned about small-appetite meals
and finger foods;
how the act of smiling can lift your mood,
and smiles are made for sharing.

Many patients have other priorities than living longer
(mine would be beer),
and, by listening closely
to our patients and their loved ones,
we can directly address their fears
while providing tailor-made care.

Think how terrifying and lonely that journey would be
if none of you were there.

We learned that life's simple pleasures
can go a long way,
whether it's drinking tea with a cup and saucer
or simply finding someone who's interested
in what you have to say.

You can use smell and touch
to trigger memories of reassurance,
while slip-on shoes and typing can so easily bring joy.
Music can produce the most delightful spark
even if it happens to be the Backstreet Boys.

As the Cookie Monster said,
'Today me will live in the moment,
unless it's unpleasant,
in which case me will eat a cookie.'

We can learn an awful lot from that creature,
so top up your emotional bank account,
'cause you simply can't pour from an empty beaker.

Find your inner safety valve,
repeat a helpful mantra;
forgive yourself as well as others;
use your sense of humour.

Spend time in nature
as if you've never seen it before.
Don't stop hunting rainbows.
Don't stop wanting more.

A diagnosis of dementia isn't the end,
but the start of a different way of living,
and, thanks to the quality care
and treatment you're giving,
more people can face the future
with a smile on their face.

This new life of adapting is never anyone's choice,
but it can be filled with opportunities.
The brain is a string of fairy lights
and, if some of them start flickering,
why be embarrassed about a complicated disease?

So look after yourselves and each other.
It's so important because
happy staff mean happier patients,
and dementia can happen to any of us.

*Written and performed at University Hospitals of Leicester
NHS Trust's Older People and Dementia Champions
Celebration Event, autumn 2019*

THE BOXER

I try to hold the Boxer's fists
as he lashes out at my frame
with the fury that won his finest fights.

I hold him still
whilst the nursing assistant tugs trousers to ankles
and wipes him by surprise
with a vigorous towel.

He glares up at me with determination
and his fists vibrate in mine.
We briskly attach his braces.

His trousers bulge with piss-proof safety
as we walk him into the lounge
and place him wobbling into his slumber chair,
where he will remain until nourished
with pre-digested food,
washed down with lactulose
and a steel spoon.

We hold his fists and wipe his face
as his coach mutters victory between the rounds.
He spits a mouthful of blood across the side of the ring,
towards the trophies at his bedside;
ageing, rigid and proud.

You can run your fingers through the dust
of all the decades gone by,
the tears, joy and fights;
and Mother Nature rasps a tortured chuckle
as the boxer tumbles from the ring,
collapses and submits.
Out for the count.

I don't understand how life can be so cruel
as to take away your hands
and leave you with the tools,

but if you look beneath the battered canvas
a soul can be found,
and, just once in a while, it sings out loud,
and you can see the former majesty
to which the trophies testify
before it fades and disappears again
as it atrophies and dies.

Every day in his mind, he's alone in that ring,
punching out at his shadow.
The shadow always wins.

And as the scorecards hit the deck,
I thank his dazed and lucky stars,
because if he ever realised where he really was…

Elderly 'challenging behaviour' ward, spring 1994

SIMONE'S BAG

4am. Everyone is in bed
and the good ship Flap is sailing through calm waters.

I drift from dorm to dorm with my torch,
buoyed by people's breathing.
It's just me and my thoughts.

You want your patients to have a restful night,
but it's important to check they're still alive
on a regular basis.
There are several ways of doing this
without waking them.

Simone has to be checked every fifteen minutes,
and she has her own room,
so, in her case, all you do
is shine your torch through the glass in her door
to where you can see her duvet rising and falling,
slowly and softly.
I can hear her snoring too,
so that's all groovy.

I carry on down the corridor,
but something doesn't feel right.
So I think, Well, better safe than sorry.
No one dies tonight.

I go back and have another look through Simone's door.
The duvet's not going up and down any more,
but she is still snoring,
so I start to walk away again,
but my instincts are screaming.

So I stop.
Eventually, I realise
that I've nursed Simone lots of times before.
In fact, I've nursed her, on and off, for years,
and I've never heard her snore.

I fly back to her room, open the door
and pull her duvet back.
Her head is covered with a plastic bag,
which she's tied round her neck with a shoelace.
I rip it open, and her entire face
is blue.
She's unresponsive.

What I thought was snoring
was actually the rattling
of the plastic going into her airway.
I call for Samira to bring the oxygen,
which we give to Simone without delay.

Eventually, her colour comes back.
She slowly sits up.
We go for a fag
and she says she's sorry.
I take the cigarette she offers,
light it with a shaking hand and say, 'Don't worry.'[3]

It's all about listening to your instincts
and learning to trust them,
'cause, whenever they make you stop,
it's usually for a reason.

You sometimes call it wrong and make people annoyed,
but, generally speaking, your instincts don't lie
– not unless you're paranoid.

Adult mental health, summer 1999

---

3. At the turn of the millennium, it was commonplace for psych nurses to smoke with their patients. The patients' smoke room was the nucleus of the ward subculture, and it hosted some of the most sublime conversations I've ever been party to. We're certainly healthier now, but I can't deny that I miss those days, especially when I see how long today's nurses are obliged to spend in their office.

'YOU DON'T HAVE TO BE IN THIS MUCH PAIN, YOU KNOW…'

I heard it through the agony,
this thing she said to me.
It was the first thing out her mouth
when she entered the bay and saw me.

It was so simple
and true,
and I knew
in that moment
that my torment was finite.
Then she gave me morphine
and it made everything alright.

I'd been writhing like a maggot for several hours.
Everyone else had shrugged their shoulders.

She made a world of difference
with that simple thing she did,
and I promised I'd try to be more like her,
if I was lucky enough to live.

Meningitis, spring 2012

ROMEO THE POLICEMAN

I first met Romeo in Tesco at Beaumont Leys.
I'd done a runner to get my nails done.
He caught me among the cheese
and I thought, This could be fun!

He was strong and dark,
with eyes like shiny raisins.
His face had been chiselled
by a celestial mason,

and, as he crashed me a ciggie,
I said, 'Hi! My name's Izzy,'
and we both made the most of our impromptu liaison.
We've arranged to meet six months from now
in the dogging spot near the railway station.

So Romeo is my handsome charmer.
His truncheon is my luncheon.
My knight in shining armour.

Group poem written with mental health inpatients, summer 2019. I'd arrived on this particular ward and the atmosphere was noticeably volatile. An absconded patient had just been brought back by the police and her anger had rubbed off on her fellow patients. Over the course of the conversation, she mentioned that she found one of the coppers quite attractive, so we decided to write him a love poem, just in case they ever met again. Thirty minutes later the atmosphere was much more convivial!

NURSING PSYCHOPATHS

The nice thing about psychopaths
is that they can be very easy to get on with.

They're usually admitted in the wake of a crisis,
with the help of some sort of emergency service,
and everyone likes them,
because they tend to be affable
and they know what to say.

Then, after one or two days,
there's a chilly turn to the ward atmosphere.
People start falling out with each other,

so you put your ear to the ground
and trace it all back to the mouth
of the aforementioned psychopath,
who is basically doing their thing.
Then all your bells go ding,

so you watch and wait,
and within another few days
the continuous affectation of basic human decency
becomes too much of an effort,
and then the mask starts to slip
and people see through it.

At that point they're even easier to get on with,
because they're losing all their allies,
so you just keep the rapport intact
and let them think you're a little bit daft,
while you conspire behind their back to organise
a discharge date,

because, in fairness to them, this place
will never ever help them face
the full implications of responsibility.
For that kind of thing you need years of therapy,

and we have twenty-nine other patients in here:
people with depression and schizophrenia,
people who are terrified inside their own skin,
people who are actively trying to do themselves in.

The last thing we need is a psychopath.
We already have enough of them on the staff.

Adult mental health, winter 1998

SWEAR TO BE HAPPY

When you wake up next to a python
and it turns out to be a poo;
you put your pants on back to front
on the way out of the loo;

you get stuck in your coat
and can't pay for things at Tesco's;[4]
your coffee's full of salt
and Siri tells you, 'Fuck knows…'

It's times like this you need to swear.
Alleviate that despair.
Shout 'twat' at anyone who'll listen.
Throw in a crafty 'prick',
then apologise for your disposition.

Call the AA
and tell them they're all wankers.
Tell the vicar he's a bellend,
and then see if he thanks yer.

If he won't give you his forgiveness,
bribe him with some pollocks,
and if he's still begrudging,
then kick him in the bollocks.

If you're pissed off,
you can swear your face off
at every knobber who crosses your path,
every dickhead who's having a laugh,
every tosser who overfills your bath,
every cockwomble who makes life an unnecessary faff.

Hold your head up high
and shout, 'Fuck off and die!'
because saying 'silly billy' is just plain daft.

---

4. This actually happened to one of the participants in this poem. We have no idea how.

Group poem written with mental health inpatients, winter 2018, after collectively deciding that swearing was good for us. As a starting point, we decided to make a list of all our favourite swearwords. Somewhere in a hospital in the East Midlands, there's a flip chart with a big list of expletives on it…

SUPERPOWER

We're going to make up a story and I'll be the scribe,
because she's in bed and too poorly to write.
I start by asking what special power she'd like.

'I'd read minds,' without any hesitation.
Whose mind would she read?
She ponders this question.
'My mum's.'

Her mum, who is at her bedside,
briefly shelves her preoccupations
and her eyes meet with mine,
as we take a moment to ponder the horrific implications
of your kids actually knowing what's going on in your mind.

'I stare across the dinner table
and I can see all Mum's thoughts.
She's entertaining herself with a Spanish ballad
while telling me to eat my salad.
She says I can't have any more lasagne
till I eat at least one tomato.

'I can see that she's scared,
even though she's smiling.
I look deeper,
and I learn
that she's concerned
about more than the tomato.
She's worried about me,
but doesn't want me to know.

'So I tell her that she makes everything okay
and, whatever happens, we'll face it together.
It's always been that way.

'And, to make the point,
I stand on the table and do a little dance

in time to the ballad in her head.
She gives me a round of applause,
smiles properly and then says,
"Yes, we can face anything together."

'I can see, though,
that she's not forgotten the tomato,
and until it's gone, there'll be no more lasagne.'

Writer in residence, paediatric ward, winter 2019

WHISKY IN YOUR TEA

Breakfast isn't what it used to be.
We used to start the day with a pork pie
and a drop of whisky in our tea.
It would give your soul a glow
and set you up for the day.
Now it's just a bowl of cornflakes,
'cause they took the whisky away.

Writer in residence, elderly ward, summer 2019

PSYCHIATRIC CRASH TEAM

My pager goes.
It's the panic alarm,
activated from ward 4,
next door.

I make my apologies to the patient I'm talking to
and leave the ward in all haste.
Someone could be legging it,
or it might be a restraint.

There again, it could be a false alarm,
and there'll be a hapless health professional
sheepishly doing a walk of shame.

Now, I'm quite tall –
six foot three, all in all –
and when I run
I'm like a gazelle trying to take off,
so I go pounding onto ward 4,
when I'm abruptly stopped
by the doorframe connecting with the top of my head.
I go flying backwards and land on the deck.

The protagonist is a patient trying to leave the ward.
He was grappling with the staff
and they were holding him back.

Upon seeing my calamity,
they all stop what they're doing.
The patient breaks free,
runs up to me,
holds out his hand
and helps me to my feet.

The nurses have the seclusion room ready
to put him in,
but, now he's de-escalated,
they stop what they're doing,

because you can't seclude a patient
who's just stopped to help a nurse.
My canny distraction technique interrupted the spiral
and stopped things getting worse.

The patient explains he wants to go to the shop
because he's run out of fags.
I go back to my ward,
collect a specimen bag.

Then I enter the smoke room
and explain to the clientele
why I have a lump on my bonce.
When they stop laughing,
I tell them about the patient next door
who's run out of fags.
Then I pass round the specimen bag,
which they fill at once
with tobacco and papers,
a panatela and some filters,
a couple of Mayfairs and Benson & Hedges –
enough to last the rest of the weekend and more.
I give them my thanks and return to ward 4

and present the patient with his emergency package.
He takes it with gratitude and promises to manage
his anger a little better when he next gets the hump.
I leave the ward smiling, rubbing my lump.

Adult mental health, spring 1998

MY EYES

My eyes have turned around
and they are burning into my brain.
I can see myself for what I am
and what, before, I have been.

I can see the me you look at
and what you want to see,
but I'll never see your face again.
All I will see is me.

Therapeutic community, summer 1994

HERMAN'S HABIT, PART 2

It's just gone midnight and I'm in a mess.
I'm in my kitchen in my underwear,
I'm sweating like a pig
and my chest
is heaving.
I need to leave the building,
but they'll spot my bid for freedom
and, before I even get to see them,
they'll split me open like a septic wound,
and I can't do a damned thing
to find out who they are
or even try to stop them.

But if I don't even try, then I'll never survive.
I grope the grime around me
and grab the carving knife.

I don't have a clue how many there are,
'cause it's dark out there and I can't see,
but if tonight's the night it all goes to shit,
then I'll take a ton of them down with me,
and whoever it is that's behind all this carnage
won't look quite so smart with their head in my fridge.

I'm going to take the fight to them.
I'm going to get out there and carve 'em up,
create mayhem!

They're going to reap what they've been sowing:
a solo one-man jihad!
Although I might ring the ward before I get going,
just in case this is all down to that speed I had…

Adult mental health, spring 2002

HERMAN'S HABIT, PART 3

Ten past three on the night shift.
Herman's crashed into it
and smashed the tranquillity
into all his horror stories.
He was terrified
when he arrived
an hour ago,
but I gave him something from my trolley
to help him get back on his.

I should be on my break, but here I sit,
hoping the meds will work a little more magic,
while Herman prattles on for what feels like forever,
each word knitting his brain back together.

'You see, what I want to know
is how you get all these enormous thoughts into one little head,
especially when they're all falling out with each other.
It's better, if you can,
to try and arrange them into some sort of priority order,
although that's easier said than done,
but that's basically bollocks,
because everything's easier said than done,
except breathing,
unless you're on a ventilator or something.
Now, the point I was going to make…
hold on, I'll start from the beginning.'

By 6am, Herman's feeling much better
and the racing thoughts have stopped,
so, because he's not felt to be sectionable,
we let him go as soon as the doors are unlocked.

'I feel much better now. Thank you.
I can't believe it was all in my mind.
It was genuinely terrifying.

It felt so real at the time.
If it's alright with you,
I'll just take the bus home,
run a hot bath,
relax and unwind.'

So Herman goes home
and takes all the rest of his speed.
Some time later, the police pull him off his roof,
where he's waving his knife
and shouting abuse at passers-by.
Now he's on a section.
I'll be seeing him tonight.

Adult mental health, spring 2002

DR BRICE

Dr Brice put her name in the wrong part of the form
and accidentally sectioned herself.
This amused us greatly,
because she was bad for people's mental health.

She went on a trip to Venice,
paid for by the drug company
that was keen to invest in her impartiality.

She changed everyone's meds when she came back.
Carnage ensued and people relapsed.
One man's mental health went so badly to shit
that he smashed up the ward
and put two nurses off sick.

So don't be like Dr Brice.
Just stick to the guidelines from NICE.

Adult mental health, spring 2002

TOM'S LOVE STORY

Well, I was doing alright
until everything went wrong.
My wife went away
and took my daughter and son,
although, to be fair,
I did have an affair.
Then I told her about it
and then they were gone,

leaving me in the suburbs
in this house full of guilt
and only the disdain of the cat for company.
Every evening I'd sit
and wonder why I did it,
and then all my regrets became bigger than me.

As the weeks went by,
I spent more time
collecting pseudo-friends online,
and that's how Serena came into my life.

Ahh, Serena.
She'd also been through a messy separation
and there was something very gentle about her,
and, even though I'd never met her
and she lived in Scandinavia,
she somehow bridged the distance
and crept into my skin.

But, although I did my best to try and be happy,
I couldn't stop missing my wife and my family.
I came to realise that without them
I'm nothing,
and, although I tried my hardest,
I still felt utterly empty.

And then I found God,

or maybe God found me.
It's hard to be sure.
It all went wonky at that point,
and my memory's still a little bit hazy,

but I discovered God and dumped Serena.
She took it really badly.
She trashed our place in cyberspace
and sent me all these messages
calling me a waste of her energy,

and then God told me she was going to get in her car
and drive away for a while
to get me out of her system,
but during the course of her journey
she'd crash and die,
and it'd all be my fault.

I run upstairs and turn on the computer.
I send her a message to try and warn her;
to stop her getting in the car,

but it's no use.
I don't know what to do.
God tells me that the message
isn't going through.
Her computer's still turned off
'cause she's packing her bags
in a bit of a strop.
She's never going to turn it on again,
'cause she'll be in a car
and she'll be dead,
and from this distance
there's not a lot
that I can do.

Then I remember something I'd said to God once
about how I'd boil my own hand to prove my loyalty.
I didn't think much about it at the time.
In fact, to be honest, I'd said it a little bit flippantly,

but maybe my connection with Serena is so tremendous
that if I were to experience a certain level of distress,
she might feel it too
and then she'd think of me.

She'd go online and get my warning.
She'd leave her car at home that morning,
and then she'd get to live,
although she'd probably still be angry.

God agrees that it's a pretty good plan,
so, on his instruction,
I fill a couple pans
with water,
one of which I bring to the boil.
The other I keep cold to put it in after.

And I boil my hand for five minutes.
I know that it's five
because I do it on the timer.

Then I take it out and put it in the cold,
which sends a shiver up my arm and into my soul,
until God tells me to take it out,
pad it dry,
wrap it in a towel
and do some housework.

To be fair, the place was a tip,
'cause over the last few days I'd really neglected it.

Then God tells me that the plan hasn't worked.
My efforts were fruitless
and Serena's still oblivious.
She's turning the ignition and starting to roll
towards her rendezvous with death.

I throw myself on the Almighty's mercy
and he sends me into the garden.

I reach the edge of the flower beds.
God tells me to unwrap my towel,
throw it over the hedge
and dig.

So now I'm digging the soil
with my hand that's been boiled
and asking His help to come to terms with the pain,
and, as my skin comes loose like a glove in that hole,
I slowly pull the last bits away,

and underneath
is what I can only describe as a new beginning:
a sense of hope
that, as long as my neighbours don't see what I'm doing,
I might just be winning the day.

But God says, 'Nope.
Serena is still on her way.'

I offer Him my soul to ravage
and He sends me crying into the garage,
straight towards the circular saw.

I switch it on and cut off my forefinger,
and then my pinkie.
Then I try to do my thumb,
but I snag it on the joint,
and I must confess
it did start to hurt at that point,

so, on God's suggestion, I pull it all free
and take my hand off at the wrist,
rather than going through the ball-ache
of doing each finger separately.

Then I hear a noise
and there's my daughter.

She's popped by
just to say hi;
sees the hand,
sees the fingers,
starts to cry,
and calls the police,
who come and take me to casualty.
That was a few weeks ago
and now I feel a little bit silly.

The doctors say I had a stress-induced psychosis,
which apparently has an excellent prognosis.
I've made a full recovery.
Sometimes it feels like it was somebody else,
but it was obviously me
and I was obviously poorly.

I'll get a new hand, but my stump feels sore,
and me and God – we're not talking any more.

So it's three in the morning and here I am.
Thanks for the lorazepam.

Today my wife and kids are coming to visit,
and if this brings us closer, it might just be worth it.

I've not contacted Serena,
but I can't help but wonder what she'd say
if she knew
that someone she'd never met
had gone through so much
to try and keep her safe.

Adult mental health, summer 1999

DUCKS

There once was a hospital duckling.
Its mum was a temporary visitor.
She made her nest in our courtyard.
She'd waddle into the bushes
and all the chicks would follow her.

They'd sleep under her wings
and peck at seeds in the trough.
We'd sometimes feed them Weetabix.
This mum had, we think, eight chicks,
but now they're down to four.
There's a lot of magpies around here
and we don't like them any more.

This duck has several nesting sites
around our hospital.
She was here this time last year,
but we didn't know if she'd return at all.

She sits and watches from a distance,
while the ducklings do what ducklings do.
Sometimes they peer at us
through the lounge window.
You're watching them
and they're watching you.

Sometimes we hear her quack,
and, although we can't hear them through the windows,
we have it on good authority
that the ducklings all quack back.

There are very few wards that can boast their own ducks,
and every morning, when we wake up,
it's a joy to see them thrive.
They've helped the smile return to our faces,
just by being alive.

Group poem written with inpatients of an elderly ward,
summer 2019

MY KINGDOM FOR A SWIPE CARD

Can I borrow your swipe card,
just for twenty minutes?
I'll guard it very carefully
and I promise I'll take care of it.

I'll bring you something from the shops,
or spend an hour by the sea.
I'll sit outside and think sensible thoughts
and come back in time for tea.

Just let me have that swipe card,
so I can check the detail.
I'll give it back immediately,
albeit via airmail.

Writer in residence, adult mental health, summer 2019

FIGHT IN THE OLD DOG

When life decides to throw you some curlers,
there's no reason or announcement.
My wife's dad died
and then I had my brain haemorrhage,
and she found herself undergoing psychiatric treatment.

They took everything off me; all my licences:
plant machinery, trade, PSB, HGV.
I used to go out and do things
and I still have lots of fight in me.

I get annoyed
when people think there's stuff that I can't do.
I'll decide that for myself, if it's okay with you.

Apart from my wife;
I take instruction from her.
Occasionally she says, 'Don't do that!'
and deep down I know she's right,
but I want to do it anyway
and it tears me up inside.

I had to be reassessed.
They were charging me a fortune for these lessons
so I could resit my driving test.
The assessor, being a touchy chap
who thinks he knows best,
said, 'You're being too cautious.

'Think less of the safety,
more of the continuity,
especially at islands.
Try and fit into the gap,
instead of waiting for what feels like years
for a larger gap in the traffic to one day appear.'

Now, traditionally
I'm not really overcautious in traffic,
but, on reflection, I had been,
mainly for his benefit.

So, we're on this double island.
The traffic's going really fast,
but I know this island very well.
I've done it plenty in the past.

So I gave him a grin and just relaxed
and slipped at speed into the gap.

He nearly had a heart attack!
He grabbed the door and spluttered and spat.

'Hold on,' I said.
'When I gave you safety first, you didn't want it,
and now you're having a coronary
'cause I've just pulled into traffic.
Make your mind up,
young pup.'

I'm pleased to report I never had to go back.

Writer in residence, art group for people with strokes and
head injuries, winter 2016

A MAN RE-EVALUATES

The old man had come from Serbia
to see his only son,
who'd been a patient on here
for the last three months.

He'd given us quite a run for our money.
Now he'd made a good recovery
and was ready to go home.
His father had travelled from Serbia alone.

He'd never left the country of his birth before,
and now he found himself in Leicester,
where everyone's a minority;
an integrated patchwork of religions and races,
going back to the textile industry.

He was enormously grateful
for what we'd done for his son,
and, because I was the nurse in charge of his care,
he thought I was something of a hero.
He tried to give me cash to express his gratitude,
and it broke my heart,
but I had to say no.

The day he goes back, we sit down for a chat.
In faltering English, he makes the point that

'I've never seen so many colours of skin
walking along the street that I'm in.
Your kids play together
and you seem to be happier.

'It's made me do a lot of thinking,
and I've realised that, whoever we are,
wherever we're from
and whatever we believe,
there is only one God
and He loves all of us all equally…'

Then, without irony,
he leans forward and says,
'Except the Jews.'

I look him in the eye, hold his gaze
and say, 'No, mate. Us too.'

In his face I see something resembling shame.
He stays quiet for a while,
then shakes my hand again
and tells me he has some more thinking to do.
We say goodbye and he leaves the room.

I stay for a moment, feeling glad I said that,
'cause even a lifelong racist can sometimes be brought back.
If hate's a wall of arseholes, he might just be the crack,
and I'm not even Jewish, but we won't worry about that.

Adult mental health, spring 2001

THE ANDREW LANSLEY RAP

Chorus:
Andrew Lansley – greedy.
Andrew Lansley – tosser.
The NHS is not for sale,
you grey-haired manky codger.

So the budget of the PCTs
he wants to hand to the GPs.
Oh, please.
Dumb geeks are gonna buy from any willing provider,
get care from private companies.
They saw the pie and they want a piece;
got their eyes on the P's like mice for the cheese.
I talk truth when I ride the beat.
You talk shite when you speak,
see money when you close your eyes to sleep.

So fall back.
Your face is like a shrivelled-up ballsack.
The stuff that you say is bullcrap.
I'm sure Andy Pandy snorts crack.

Health minister – I mean 'sinister'.
You know your public will finish yer.
Is your brain really that miniature?
You're full of crap.
Give yourself an enema.

Made filthy rich
by those who represent Walkers Crisps,
Mars and Pizza Hut;
proved you're a health slut
and you're always talking shit.

A hundred and thirty-four pounds an hour.
Every week, that's quite a lot of quids,
and you came to the conclusion
that the food industry could be a little less strict.

Scandal disclosed that you flipped your second home.
You said your claims were within the rules,
filled your pockets, took us for fools.

So how would you cope
when folk get ill, injured and broke,
but don't have the dough
to get their life back on the road,
so poor die slow
and the rich take control?

(Chorus)

Lansley's white paper 'Liberating the NHS'
sets out a plan where we'll become more like the US
and care will be farmed out to private companies,
who will sell their service to the NHS via GPs,
who will have more to do
with service purchase arrangements
than anything to do with seeing their patients.

He's been given cash
by John Nash,
chairman of Care UK:
a private healthcare provider
who, if they have their way,
will be the biggest beneficiaries
of Conservative Lib Dem policies
to privatise healthcare and pull apart the welfare state.

These plans have been slagged by patient organisations,
charities and unions,
nursing and medical institutions.
The Royal College of GPs even joined the attack,
looked closely at the proposals
and said they were crap.

So say yes for the NHS.
Andrew Lansley can suck on David Cameron's breast.
His quest is for the rich to pay less,
and the poor have to stress;
it'll be one big mess.

(Chorus)

*Co-written with MC NxtGen as a response to the then health
secretary Andrew Lansley's white paper, spring 2011. To see
the video, enter 'Andrew Lansley Rap' into YouTube.*

RICHARD'S LEAVES

Sunday afternoon.
There are no doctors or OTs.
The ward is only three quarters full.
Quite a few patients are out on leave.

I'm walking around the hospital grounds
with Richard – a retired botanist.
He wants to collect some leaves for rubbing,
but he's not been allowed off the ward until now.
He doesn't know why,
and I won't tell him.

Three days earlier, he had attacked me.
He was stark naked
and acutely psychotic.
It was triggered by a urine infection.
It improved quickly with antibiotics,
and, praise be, he has no recollection.

It all seems a very long time ago
this crispy autumn Sunday.
Richard's much better,
but he's still on a section,
and this short escorted time outside
is entirely down to my discretion.

We return to the ward with a bagful of leaves,
talking about botany.
As we approach the nursing station,
Richard turns to me.

'They won't think I'm mad
for collecting leaves, will they, Rob?'

'Only if you start eating them, Richard.'

We both giggle as we pass the obs desk
and go our separate ways.
I pay homage to the god of paperwork,
while he sits with a smile and rubs leaves all day.

Adult mental health, autumn 1994

LOCKDOWN HAIKU

I was once a nurse
who left to be a poet.
Now I've come back home.

Spring 2020

POST-MEAL LOCKDOWN POEM

When this lockdown finishes,
I'm going straight to the pub.
I'll see my nearest and dearest
and give them a massive hug.

I'll pop over to McDonald's
and scoff a big McFlurry.
I'll visit Desford bird park
and I won't be in a hurry
to leave any time soon.
I'll walk over the hills
and watch the sun come up,
and then I'll watch the moon.

I'll see my baby niece
and bounce her on my knee,
and she'll drown me in a mix
of carrots and mushy peas.

I'll go wandering with my camera
and take photographs of nature.
I'll do a tour of the safari parks
and maybe Butlin's later.

I'll go on a picnic with the friends that I like best,
and once a week on Thursday
I'll still applaud the NHS.

I'll take myself on holiday, away to Timbuktu,
or maybe Greece, Croatia, Coalville or just Corfu.

I'll go clubbing and see bands,
and dance around at festivals.
I'll fly to the States, see Donald Trump
and kick him in the testicles.

I'll go to the IMAX and treat myself to Mulan,
then order a Chinese takeaway,
as long as it's not from Wuhan.

I'll continue to shake my head
at the conspiracy theory myths.
I'll have a party with my family,
but not the ones I live with.

I'll go skipping with my friends
through the cities and the sticks,
but many weeks will pass
before I tune in again to Netflix.

I'll take a trip to Poundland
and stock up on my stuff,
but I won't bulk buy any bog roll,
because I really have enough.

When this isolation finally ends,
we'll enjoy freedom at long last.
Forget about burning bras –
I'll incinerate this mask!

*Group poem written with eating disorder inpatients, spring
2020. I'd returned to nursing and this poem was written as
part of post-meal distraction.*

LITTLE VICTORIES

When they remember the tray in your commode,
so you don't dump on the floor,
you feel happy at life's triumphs
and it leaves you wanting more.

When you find some paper in your pocket
and it turns out to be a fiver;
you accidentally miss the therapy group
and no one thinks you're a skiver.

When the storeroom's left unlocked
and it seems to be well-stocked
and there's no staff in the vicinity,
there's no reason to stop
temptation taking over me,
so I don the PPE
and then I take a selfie.
The staff were 'very disappointed',
but it was a little victory.

When you're playing Bananagrams
and you're on that tense last letter,
and your opponent picks a 'Q'
and they don't have a 'U',
life doesn't get much better.

When you've had an apple in the dining room
for twenty consecutive days
and at last you get a banana,
things are finally going your way.

Life's little victories can help your mental health,
like when your psychiatrist fills the form out wrong
and somehow sections herself.

Racing office chairs along the highway of the ward
and shooting staff with water pistols
stops us getting bored.

When you fill a 60ml syringe and aim it with precision
at your well-meaning key worker
when they make a bad decision.

It's a lovely little victory
when they go on annual leave,
so you get a week's reprieve;

when the sun is shining,
so you can go on the group walk;
when you figure out the TV cables,
so you can finally watch the football;
when they double-check your height
and you find you're standing tall;
but I've discovered that recovery
is the best little victory of all.

Group poem written with eating disorder inpatients, summer 2020, as part of post-meal distraction. The avid reader might recognise the reference to the psychiatrist sectioning herself from the earlier poem 'Dr Brice'. Yep – in my efforts to contribute, I plagiarised myself.

LEAVING

The time has come for me to leave.
My discharge date has been agreed:
a strange new world outside the doors
unlocked, decisions left up to me.

I don't need a hot drink at half past three,
now my future's looking bright.
On my own I can finally pee.
No more torches in the night.

The first thing I'll do is drive my car
over a pile of Alpen bars.
There's nothing duller
than another Müller.[5]
I should measure my milk,
but I can't be arsed.

The community spirit will be sorely missed,
and, of course, post-meal distraction;
even when there were just a few of us,
we were always the main attraction.

I'll miss the laughs
and the regular staff –
even Rob, though his jokes are naff –
and guessing the faces behind the masks.
With this ode, my bags are packed,

so off I go.
So long, lovely people.
I've restored some weight,
but you've lightened the load.
As I continue my journey
to wherever it might lead,

---

5. Alpen bars and Müller Corners could be prescribed regularly as part of one's meal plan.

I can take my recovery
along a new road.

Group poem written with eating disorder inpatients, spring 2020, as part of post-meal distraction. One of the participants was due for discharge the following day.

NIGHT OUT

I'm in a nightclub with my friends – my colleagues.
We've got thirty beds and forty-six patients,
so tonight we're drinking heavily.

Everyone's there, apart from Lucy,
who threw up outside the chippy.
Then she slipped over on the ice
and twisted her knee.

Unbeknown to us, Lucy is now in a cubicle in A&E,
swearing drunkenly at anyone who comes near her.

Unbeknown to Lucy,
in the cubicle next to hers
is a regular patient of ours,
who's in after an overdose.
He hears Lucy swearing and immediately knows
whose voice it is.
He tells us all about it later on.
Cue several shifts of us taking the piss.

So we're all having a bit of a dance
and this woman I don't know comes up
and shakes my hand.

She says, 'Hello, Rob.
You probably won't remember me.
You nursed me a few years ago.
I wasn't at my best.
It was like I was trapped in a horror movie.
My mind was such a mess.

'I told you I wanted to be a hairdresser
and you encouraged me to seek out some kind of training.
I now own three salons, and I just saw you dancing
and wanted to say thanks,
and if you ever want your head polishing…'

Then she disappears
into the throng from where she came.
I don't remember nursing her,
which makes me sad in a way,
because I'd obviously had an impact.
I wonder how many others
have vanished from my memory.
After so many years, it's hard to keep track.

Then I realise that we meet people
at the point their crisis peaks.
They might be with us for a few days,
months or weeks,
and in that time
you do your best to be their guide
as they stumble away from torment,
back towards life,

and then they leave,
and, for the most part,
you've no idea how it pans out for them
after you've parted company.
You've just shared that little part of each other's journey,

and it teaches you to enjoy
the glorious nowness of the moment,
because once in a while
a conspiracy of circumstances
will come and kick the crap
out of your happy-ever-afters,
and everything'll go wrong,
and then you meet us.

Bummer.

Summer 2002

REFLECTIONS ON COVID

Compiled and edited from a series of group poems written with staff from Leicestershire Partnership NHS Trust, via video conference, between September and November 2020.

Part One: The Adjustment

The NHS was a lumbering juggernaut.
Then we suddenly became a speedboat.
We had to adjust rapidly just to stay afloat
and ride the tsunami of demand that came at such a speed;
trying to stay balanced, dragged along on sinking skis.

In the beginning, the fear was palpable,
yet everyone stepped up and procurement were remarkable.
There's improved connection now between enabling and
    clinical,
which hasn't always been there, at the risk of sounding cynical.

I came out of retirement and returned to the wards.
Things are very different now to how they were before.
It's the first time I've worn a uniform since I was in training.
I don't have to decide what to wear any more.

Part Two: The Impact

We've had some strange requests through the self-referral
    system.
I'd give you some examples,
but it would take too long to list them.

My clients have really struggled without the in-person contact.
They've sunk so far in isolation it's hard to get them back.

We've all found that frustrating.
They needed the therapy at the time of referral,
but after so many months of waiting
it takes longer to get better,

so sod off, sodding COVID,
and stay sodded off forever.

You're robbing people of the memories
of the last years of their lives.
Several of mine say it's worse than in the war,
'cause at least back then you could socialise.

Even a few weeks ago,
you could be someone's first face-to-face contact in months.
You'd want to chat forever, just to help alleviate the misery
of their feeling so lonely and down in the dumps.

Others with anxiety have actually been okay.
They can hide behind their masks
and they don't have people calling round all day.

Carers couldn't receive the respite they need.
We've fielded endless referrals from care homes on their knees,
begging for assistance for those who can't isolate
and keep leaving their rooms with impaired mental states.

Everyone in the care sector was woefully let down.
They've never been properly recognised,
but without the work they do
our caseload would be five times the size.

You do domestic visits,
where you're sitting sweating buckets
in apron, mask and gloves.
People sit you in their conservatories,
where the sun bakes you from above,
and the mask makes you spotty,
which leaves you feeling grotty,
but I'm still here doing this job that I love.

In order to protect my patients,
I had to send my family away;
and people became complacent.

They thought it wasn't as bad as the news portrayed.

My colleagues are now my family,
because they understand the feeling
of going in every day to find yourself dealing
with this workload whilst trying to be the perfect nurse.
We're running to keep up and things might be getting worse.

We're maintaining high standards, but they come at a price.
We're having to choose and prioritise
between mental health and COVID.
It makes me feel livid.

I can't hug a patient whose father is dying,
in case I infect him and his family,
so sod off, sodding COVID.
You're taking our humanity.

We cope in our different ways
to try and make things better.
When a patient asked me, 'Are you okay?'
I realised we are in it together.

All the psychosocial interventions are much harder to do.
There are so many more in need you have to get to,
but the team have been fantastic.
They've helped to see me through,
and we do get ten percent off at B&Q.

Part Three: Working from Home

I wasn't expecting my hair to grow so much longer,
to be banned from doing the conga,
or that I'd try and shed corona stones by panting to Jane Fonda.

When you work from home in lockdown,
all your socialising stops.
I've tried expanding my horizons
while confined to my laptop.

Different versions of me have learned to share the same space.
My home was once a happy place.
Now it's an office and I miss the folk around me.
I need the human contact to keep myself healthy.

We don't have those corridor conversations
when we're not there in the flesh,
so it's harder to have your colleagues' back
or see when they're upset.

The team meetings sound like séances,
with phrases like 'Are you with us?'
and, although I really shouldn't boast,
I'm amazed at how quickly I can nip to the loo
while making eggs on toast.

I was expecting a six-week lockdown,
but now it feels like it won't end.
I wasn't expecting the postman to be my new best friend.

You're on mute… Sorry, you're on mute…

Part Four: Reflections

In Leicester we've been in lockdown longer than anyone else.
We're more disconnected, but we're here delivering health.

Back in the spring, we were applauded but not equipped.
Now the stress is hitting hard and more of us are going sick,
and our caseload keeps expanding,
but it's harder now to meet it.

We have to create a plan to reintegrate
services that never actually stopped in the first place.
There are four different documents that duplicate
the same basic process.
You can't pass wind unless it's been risk-assessed.

There's a different sticker for every occasion,
and the hamster wheel might not get you far,
but it's good for circulation.

We now have yellow arrows on the floor,
disinfectant on the doors,
socially distanced masked-up queues
because only one at a time is allowed in the loo.

The backbone through this crisis has been the staff in admin,
who've delivered since day one and helped us to keep going.

We were fortunate enough to have redeployed staff
who had so much to offer, and, now they've gone back,
we all have greater insight into how each other works,
and at some point in the future we should have some more of that.

The big silver lining
that helped to keep us smiling
was all the goodwill from the public,
much of which translated
into chocolates and doughnuts.
We were inundated!

We had some unique offers,
like the brolly/hat combo
for seeing our patients in their gardens in the rain and snow,
or the raincoat disguised as a duck.
With some luck,
we can wear them with a smile
as we waddle through this treacle
and emerge from this experience
as robust, unflappable people.

Part Five: Handy Hints for the New Abnormal

There are several things that can brighten up your day.
A good chat with added banter can go a very long way.
A cup of quality coffee with an ear ready to listen;

the ability to give yourself permission
to take a breath and pause in the face of all the pressure.
Give yourself a break and you'll come back so much fresher.

Do something creative, like doodling on the sly.
Help each other to laugh a lot,
and, if you can't laugh, then have a good cry.

Share important occasions with colleagues when you can.
We all have celebrations,
whether it's your mum's dog's birthday
or you've found your missing nan.

We're social animals and we belong in our natural packs,
so remember we're doing well simply to adapt.

So now winter is on its way and all of us are braced.
Half the shelves in Asda were empty yesterday.
We won't take anything for granted again in the future,
and, when this is all over, we need a National Hug Day.

Till then, we'll pull together,
whatever the future brings,
so strap yourselves in for winter!
We'll party in the spring.

ABBREVIATIONS AND TERMS

A&E   Accident and Emergency

BMA   British Medical Association

LRI   Leicester Royal Infirmary

NHS   National Health Service

NICE   National Institute for Health and Care
                Excellence

OT   Occupational Therapist

P45   Document given to an employee upon
                termination of employment

PPE   Personal Protective Equipment

Section 3   Compulsory admission for mental health
                treatment lasting up to six months

ACKNOWLEDGEMENTS

'Chronic Obstructive Pulmonary Disease Singalong' was commissioned for the Leicester City Clinical Commissioning Group (CCG) via Big Difference Company, 2014.

'The Kindness of Paul' and 'Fight in the Old Dog' were first published in *Pig on the Wall*, Mantle Lane Press, 2017.

'Play the Fool Who's Fooling You' and 'I'm on a Section, Get Me Out of Here' were first published in *Word Round: Poems from Psych Wards*, Word Poetry, 2020.

'Squaddies' was first published in *Poems for Freedom*, Freedom Press, 2013.

'The NHS: A History' originated from poems commissioned for Managers in Partnership (MiP), via Big Difference Company, 2012 to 2015.

'The Andrew Lansley Rap' was commissioned by Unison, via Big Difference Company, 2011.

'Swear to Be Happy', 'Romeo the Policeman' and 'My Kingdom for a Swipe Card' were written as part of the Creative Minds and Poetry and Art for Wellbeing projects, administered by BrightSparks Arts in Mental Health in collaboration with Leicestershire Partnership NHS Trust, 2018/19.

'Whisky in Your Tea' and 'Ducks' were written as part of the Elder Tree project, administered by Writing East Midlands in collaboration with Leicestershire Partnership NHS Trust, 2019.

'Post-Meal Lockdown Poem' was first published in *Lockdown Poetry*, Freyla Press, 2020, under the title 'Mental Health Lockdown Poem'.

'Elsie's Letter' is the opening salvo of *Forget Me Not: The Alzheimer's Whodunnit*, Mantle Lane Press, 2016.

Versions of 'Home', 'A Very Chilled Robbery', 'Simone's Bag', 'Duncan's Jab', 'Tom's Love Story', 'Medication', 'Herman's Habit' and the Cassandra poems are all in the solo show Fruitcake: *Ten Commandments from the Psych Ward*.

Love and thanks to everyone involved in performance poetry, live literature, spoken word, stand-up poetry, whatever we call it, the international fringe movement and the world of rural touring. Thank you for being there.

Enormous thanks to Steve, Glenda, Gem, Sal and Lydia for their critical eyes; everyone at Burning Eye, not least for immortalising the work of so many of my favourite poets and performers; and my partner, Gemma, for filling my life with laughter and helping me evolve – it's an ongoing process!

Extra special thanks to Sallie Varnam for making everything possible.